SOGGY SEMOLINA

The School Dinners Joke Book

What's yellow and wobbly and wears dark glasses?

What's brown and squeaks when covered in milk?

Answers exclusively in SOGGY SEMOLINA – but don't show the dinner ladies!

Other Knight books you may enjoy:

THE INTER GALACTIC JOKE BOOK
Ann Droid

HOW TO HALT A HICCUP
Mary Danby

THE RIGHT IMPRESSION
Gary Wilmot

SOGGY SEMOLINA - THE SCHOOL DINNERS JOKE BOOK

BY EGON CHIPS

Illustrated by
Jeremy Tapscott

KNIGHT BOOKS
Hodder and Stoughton

British Library C.I.P.

Chips, Egon
  Soggy semolina: the school dinners joke book.
  I. Title II. Tapscott, Jeremy
  827.914

ISBN 0-340-52905-9

Typeset by Rowland Phototypesetting Ltd., Bury St Edmunds, Suffolk. Printed and bound in Great Britain for Hodder and Stoughton Paperbacks, a division of Hodder and Stoughton Ltd., Mill Road, Dunton Green, Sevenoaks, Kent TN13 2YA. (Editorial Office: 47 Bedford Square, London WC1B 3DP) by Clays Ltd. St. Ives, plc.

Knock, knock.
   Who's there?
Cereal.
   Cereal who?
Cereal pleasure to meet you all.

What do you get if you cross a piece of toast with an egg and an eiderdown?
Breakfast in bed.

What three things must you never eat at breakfast time?
Dinner, lunch and tea.

What's brown, and squeaks when covered with milk?
Mice Krispies.

What do you get if you cross bacon with a space ship?
An unidentified frying object.

What's brown on both sides and 200 metres high?
The Toast Office Tower.

What's the best day to cook bacon and eggs?
Fry day.

What do you get if you cross a pig with a naked athlete?
Streaky bacon.

What do witches like to eat for breakfast?
Rice Krispies – because they go snap, cackle and pop.

What do you get if you cross a budgie with a lawnmower?
Shredded tweet.

What do you get if you cross food with a pair of roller skates?
Meals on wheels.

FRIEND: Does your family keep the kitchen clean?
BOY: Are you joking? When the toast pops out of the toaster, it takes an hour to find it!

Did you hear the story about the Shredded Wheat and the Cornflakes?
I can't tell you how it finished because it's a serial.

What do vampires eat for breakfast?
Ready neck.

What's a termite's favourite breakfast?
Oak meal.

What sort of shoes do cornflakes wear?
K'logs.

What's the difference between a unicorn and a large lettuce?
One is a funny beast, the other is a bunny feast.

What do you get if you cross a duck with a breakfast cereal?
Quacker Oats.

What do French children eat for breakfast?
Huit heures bix.

GRANNY: If you don't eat your porridge you won't grow up to be a beautiful lady.
GIRL: Didn't *you* eat *your* porridge then, Granny?

What's a ghoul's favourite breakfast?
Dreaded Wheat.

What sort of breakfast do comedians prefer?
Cornflakes.

What's the difference between stork and butter?
Butter can't stand on one leg.

FRIEND: I've heard there are always grounds in your sister's coffee.
BOY: Enough grounds for a divorce!

What do elves bake bread with?
Elf-raising flour.

There was a young lady named Perkins
Who was so very fond of gherkins
One day at tea
She ate fifty-three
And pickled her internal workings.

What's the difference between a man who makes £5 notes and a glutton?
One is a good forger, the other is a food gorger.

RUDE BOY: My father offered to cook dinner and asked me what I'd like. I told him a life insurance policy.

Why did the lazy man get a job in the bakery?
Because he wanted a good loaf.

Why is bread like champagne?
It's good for toasting.

Why are bakers good people?
Because they earn an honest crust.

What did the flour say when it fell over?
'Don't pick me up – I'm self-raising.'

Why do bakers work so hard?
Because they knead the dough.

Will you tell me the joke about the butter?
I'd better not, you might spread it.

What's the best butter in the world?
A goat.

Why did the boy throw the butter out of the window?
Because he wanted to see the butterfly.

There was a young lady of Lynn
Who was so uncommonly thin
That when she essayed
To drink lemonade
She slipped through the straw and fell in.

RUDE GIRL: My dad and mum have a great partnership.
FRIEND: How's that?
RUDE GIRL: He earns the bread and she burns it.

PUPIL: Miss, have you heard the joke about the three eggs?
COOKERY TEACHER: No.
PUPIL: Two bad!

RUDE GIRL: This canteen must have a very clean kitchen.
SCHOOL COOK: Thank you. What makes you say that?
RUDE GIRL: Everything tastes of soap.

An old lady who came from Kilbride
Ate so many apples she died;
The apples fermented
Inside the lamented
Making cider inside 'er inside.

What's the difference between an elephant and a biscuit?
Ever tried dunking an elephant in your tea?

FATHER: Before we were married your mother turned my head with her good looks.
RUDE BOY: Now she turns your stomach with her bad cooking.

COOKERY TEACHER: What's the best way to serve leftovers?
PUPIL: To somebody else.

PUPIL: My dad's motorbike can cook eggs.
COOKERY TEACHER: Really? What type of motorbike is it?
PUPIL: A scrambler.

RUDE BOY: My sister has burned so much bread our toaster has been declared a fire hazard.

Knock, knock.
  Who's there?
Buddha.
  Buddha who?
Buddha this slice of bread for me, will you?

How can you spot an idiot on an oil-rig?
He's the one throwing bread to the helicopters.

Why do bees have sticky hair?
Because they have honey combs.

What do you get if you cross a chicken with a kangaroo?
Pouched eggs.

What did the mother bee say to the baby bee?
'Don't be naughty, honey, just beehive yourself while I comb your hair.'

There was a young man from Leeds
Who swallowed a packet of seeds;
Within just one hour
His nose was a flower
And his head was a riot of weeds.

COOKERY TEACHER: What's a good way of keeping your food bills down?
PUPIL: Using a heavier paperweight.

What do you get if you cross a jar of jam with an elephant?
Sandwiches that don't forget.

A glutton who lived on the Rhine
Was asked at what time he would dine;
He replied, 'At eleven,
At three, five and seven,
At eight and a quarter past nine.'

What's the difference between a greedy person
and a grill?
One takes most, the other makes toast.

COOKERY TEACHER: How can we prevent
food from going bad?
PUPIL: By eating it.

What did the monster eat after the dentist took all his teeth out?
The dentist.

'Mummy, mummy, there's a man at the door selling honey.'
'Tell him to buzz off.'

Knock, knock.
  Who's there?
Zombies.
  Zombies who?
Zombies make honey, others are queens.

What do you get if you cross a ghost with a packet of crisps?
Snacks that go crunch in the night.

Did you hear about the idiot who tried to kill himself by taking an overdose of aspirins?
After two he felt better.

What's the difference between a young lady and a fresh loaf?
One is a well-bred maid, the other is well-made bread.

FATHER TO SON: You eat like a pig. Do you know what a pig is?
RUDE BOY: Yes, Dad – a hog's son.

What do you get if you cross a mouse with a bar of soap?
Bubble and squeak.

Why do idiots eat biscuits?
Because they're crackers.

Why did the boy put a slice of bread in his comic?
Because he liked crumby jokes.

What's the difference between a market gardener and an actor?
One minds his peas, the other minds his cues.

What do you call a fatherless Rice Krispy?
Snap, crackle, no pop.

What's a vampire's favourite fruit?
Neck-tarines.

What do you find in a haunted cellar?
Whines and spirits.

Knock, knock.
  Who's there?
Lydia.
  Lydia who?
Lydia teapot is cracked.

A Diet of Dotty Definitions

Apricot   Bed for a small monkey.

Baked Beans on Toast   Skinheads on a raft.

Beetroot	A potato with very high blood pressure.
Cauliflower	The blossom a sheep dog wears in his buttonhole.
Celery	Money you get for working.
Coconut	Someone who is mad about chocolate.
Fish Fingers	A handy kind of food.
Grape	A gooseberry with a skinhead hair style.
Gooseberry	Fruit eaten by geese.
Ice Cream	Yell at the top of your voice.
Mushroom	School canteen.
Mustard	The only substance that stays hot in a fridge.
Noodle Soup	Nourishment for the brain.
Oyster	What you shout when you want someone to lift up your mother.
Prune	A plum that's seen better days.

Quince	Five children born at the same time.
Rhubarb	Bloodshot celery.
Runner Bean	A fast vegetable.

Sago	How you start a pudding race.
Snack	A refresher course.
Walnut	A screw to drive into the wall.
Water	Thirst aid.

What cheese is made backwards?
Edam.

'Waiter, will my hamburger be long?'
'*No sir, it will be round and flat.*'

Is it true that carrots are good for the eyesight?
Well, you never see rabbits wearing glasses.

FRIEND: Some people can cook but don't.
RUDE BOY: Our school cook can't cook but does!

Knock, knock.
    Who's there?
Olive.
    Olive who?
Olive just round the corner.

PUPIL: Could I have a horrible shrivelled up fried egg with hairs on it, some cold greasy chips and some rock hard peas, please?
CANTEEN LADY: I don't serve food like that.
PUPIL: Well, you did yesterday.

RUDE PUPIL: What's this?
CANTEEN LADY: It's bean soup.
RUDE PUPIL: I don't care what it's been, what is it now?

What is Count Dracula's favourite snack?
A fangfurter.

How do monsters like their shepherd's pie?
Made with real shepherds.

How do Daleks deal with eggs?
They eggs-terminate them.

Knock, knock.
  Who's there?
Exam.
  Exam who?
Eggs, ham and cheese.

There were two eggs boiling in a saucepan. One said, 'Phew, it's hot in here.' The other egg said, 'Wait till you get out, you'll get your head bashed in.'

COOKERY TEACHER: At a buffet party, should one serve boiled eggs?
PUPIL: One should serve whoever shows up.

What's served in glasses and is difficult to drink?
A stiff drink.

What's alcoholic and very, very difficult to drink?
A gin and cement.

MOTHER: This tea is terrible.
FATHER: I made it in my pyjamas.
MOTHER: No wonder it tastes so bad.

How do chickens start a race?
From scratch.

FRIEND: Last year my mum served a special turkey for Christmas and everyone was absolutely tickled.
RUDE BOY: Forgot to remove the feathers, did she?

POLITE GIRL: Is it good manners to eat chicken with your fingers?
RUDE BOY: No, you should eat your fingers separately.

What made the boy turkey fall in love with the girl turkey?
She egged him on.

Why are turkeys wiser than chickens?
Ever heard of Kentucky Fried Turkey?

What do you call a cheese and egg pie that breaks down doors?
A bionic flan.

What sort of roles do actors like?
Macbeth, King Lear and cheese and onion.

What's the difference between a dinosaur and a sandwich?
A sandwich doesn't weigh ten tons.

MOTHER: What did you have for dinner at school today?
RUDE GIRL: A mixture of modern technology and past history.
MOTHER: What on earth was that?
RUDE GIRL: Micro-chips in ancient grease.

What happened when the fish fought the chips?
The fish got battered.

Who sits on the bottom of the sea and makes you an offer you can't refuse?
The Codfather.

What's warm, greasy and romantic?
Chips that pass in the night.

What do monsters eat at sea?
Fish and ships.

SCHOOL COOK: I have stewed liver, boiled tongue and frogs' legs.
RUDE PUPIL: Don't tell me your problems, just give me my lunch.

RUDE BOY: I must say, the meals at our school give food for thought.
FRIEND: Really?
RUDE BOY: Well they're certainly not fit for eating!

RUDE PUPIL TO CANTEEN LADY: What's this on my plate, just in case I have to describe it to the school doctor?

Why was the corn stalk angry with the farmer?
The farmer kept pulling its ears.

What do you get if you cross a bottle of
lemonade with a masseur?
A fizzy o'therapist.

How do you make ginger wine?
Twist his arm up his back.

If you raise corn in dry weather, what do you
raise in wet weather?
An umbrella.

Why did the idiot put corn in his shoes?
Because of his pigeon toes.

'That new restaurant for idiots has an
interesting item on the menu.'
'Oh, *what's that?*'
'Soup in a basket.'

Knock, knock.
   Who's there?
Soup.
   Soup who?
Souperman.

RUDE BOY TO SCHOOL COOK: I asked for some soup 20 minutes ago — are you having trouble opening the tin?

FRIEND: This is good soup.
RUDE PUPIL Yes, it sounds good.

What's hot, greasy and steals cattle?
A *beef burglar*.

Why doesn't Count Dracula like eating in restaurants?
He worries about getting a steak through the heart.

SCHOOL COOK: How did you find your beefburger, sonny?
RUDE PUPIL: With a magnifying glass.

What do you get if you cross a church choir with a quarter pound of mince?
A hymnburger.

What do you get if you cross a house with a quarter pound of mince?
A homeburger.

RUDE PUPIL TO SCHOOL COOK: Is this steak well done, or has it been cremated?

Delicious Insults for the
School Dinner Lady . . .

★ Can I take one of these dumplings home? I need a new cricket ball.

★ Can I take home a barrow load of this treacle tart? My dad wants to lay a new garden path.

★ This fly looks extremely well-cooked.

★ May I have another plate for the maggots?

- ★ Did you kill this cabbage yourself?
- ★ The sauce looks very artistic – just like paint.
- ★ What kind of eggs are these – pterodactyl's?
- ★ I know the fish fingers are dead, but there was no need to cremate them.
- ★ Are those sultanas, or do you keep rabbits under the counter?
- ★ Are these sesame seeds, or have you been picking your nose?

RUDE PUPIL: I bet we've got salad for lunch today.
CANTEEN LADY: That's right. How did you know?
RUDE PUPIL: I couldn't smell anything burning.

What's the difference between a mouldy lettuce and a dismal song?
One is a bad salad, the other is a sad ballad.

What do you call a man who can sing and drink lemonade at the same time?
A pop singer.

What's yellow and fills fields with music?
Popcorn.

Where did the baby ear of corn come from?
The stalk brought him.

What's small and furry and cuts corn?
A combine hamster.

CHILD: I don't like cheese with holes in it.
MOTHER: Just eat the cheese then and leave
the holes on the side of your plate.

What's yellow, brown and hairy?
Cheese on toast dropped on the carpet.

What do you get if you cross a cowboy with a stew?
Hopalong Casserole.

COOKERY TEACHER: I made a beef casserole and the school cat has just eaten it.
PUPIL: Never mind, miss, we can easily get another cat.

What's a ghost's favourite dinner?
Ghoulash.

What's a ghost's second favourite dinner?
Spook-hetti.

What's the difference between an elephant and spaghetti?
Elephants don't slip off the end of your fork.

If cheese comes after dinner, what comes after cheese?
Mice.

CANTEEN LADY: And after your main course, what will you have to follow?
PUPIL: If it's anything like yesterday's meal, I'll probably have indigestion.

FRIEND: My school meals melt in your mouth.
RUDE GIRL: Too bad the cook doesn't defrost them first.

What makes cooks cruel?
They beat eggs, whip cream and batter fish.

What is the motto of fish friers?
If at first you don't succeed, fry, fry again.

What is hot, greasy, and makes you unhappy?
A chip on the shoulder.

Who plays the bagpipes while cooking fish and chips?
The Frying Scotsman.

What do you get if you cross a hamburger with a Scotsman?
A Big Mac.

'Doctor, doctor, I feel like a fish.'
'You poor sole, plaice yourself on the couch.'

What's the best thing to put into a hamburger?
Your teeth.

PUPIL: Excuse me, why have you got your finger on my beefburger?
SCHOOL COOK: To stop it falling on the floor again.

WAITER: How do you like your steak, sir?
RUDE BOY: Big.

'Twas in a restaurant they met,
Romeo and Juliet;
He had no cash to pay the debt,
So Romeo'd what Juliet.

RUDE BOY: How much is lunch at this restaurant?
WAITER: Twenty pounds a head, sir.
RUDE BOY: Just bring me an ear, then.

Who wrote Great Eggspectations?
Charles Chickens.

What do you get if you cross a hen with a poodle?
Pooched eggs.

If an egg came floating down the River Thames, where would it have come from?
A chicken.

Who conquered half the world, laying eggs along the way?
Attila the Hen.

Knock, knock.
   Who's there?
Egbert.
   Egbert who?
Egbert no bacon.

What tells jokes and lays eggs?
A comedihen.

What do you get if you cross a hyena with an Oxo cube?
An animal that makes a laughing stock of itself.

RUDE PUPIL'S COMMENT ON IRISH STEW: Ah, the policeman's favourite meal — Irish stew in the name of the law.

'I've lost my turkey. What should I do?'
'*Call the Flying Squad.*'

What do you get if you cross a bottle of lemonade with Orville?
Duck's Fizz.

What did the tonic water say to the gin?
'Diluted to meet you.'

What do you get if you cross a hen with a banjo?
A chicken that plucks itself.

What is a turkey's favourite TV programme?
The feather forecast.

RUDE PUPIL TO SCHOOL COOK: Is this rice or were they maggots?

RUDE PUPIL TO SCHOOL COOK: Can you take this away, please. I think it's the same meal I rejected the last time I was here.

RUDE PUPIL TO SCHOOL COOK: Has the electricity been cut off? I asked for a hot meal.

RUDE PUPIL TO SCHOOL COOK: Do you serve indigestion tablets with every course?

RUDE PUPIL: What do I have to do to get a glass of water in this place?
SCHOOL COOK: Set yourself on fire.

CANTEEN LADY: Eat your cabbage, it's full of iron.
PUPIL: So that's why it's so tough.

CLANG!

RUDE PUPIL: I don't like the way you've made this pie.
CANTEEN LADY: What? I'll have you know I was making pies before you were born.
RUDE PUPIL: I think this is one of them.

What do you get if you cross a potato with a sponge?
A vegetable that soaks up lots of gravy.

Why shouldn't you tell secrets in a vegetable garden?
Because corn has ears.

I eat peas with honey
I've done it all my life;
They do taste kind of funny
But it keeps them on the knife.

GIRL: Did you know there was an accident in the school canteen yesterday?
RUDE PUPIL: Yes I know – I had it for my lunch.

TEACHER: John, Why are you the only child in class today?
JOHN: Because I was the only one who didn't have a school dinner yesterday.

RUDE PUPIL'S COMMENT ON COTTAGE PIE: I know you're a perfectionist, but there was no need to put thatch on it.

St. Pizza's High School
MENU

deathlist

Available NOW in the Dining Room! —
execution chamber

suspicion and trash →
SAUSAGES AND MASH

FAGGOTS
maggot meatballs

EGG AND CHIPS
eyeball and soggy fingers

BEEF BURGERS AND CHIPS
Fried bathmats + dead slugs in axle grease

drainpipes in Poly filla →
MACARONI CHEESE

TOMATO JUICE
Dracula's blood

worms in sewage
SPAGHETTI BOLOGNAISE

SWEETS
Sours ←

CHOCOLATE CUSTARD
radioactive effluent

TAPIOCA
frog spawn

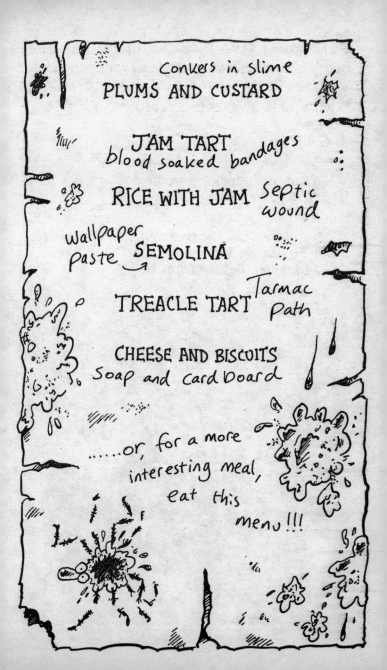

Conkers in Slime
PLUMS AND CUSTARD

JAM TART
blood soaked bandages

RICE WITH JAM Septic
wound

Wallpaper
paste **SEMOLINA**

TREACLE TART Tarmac
Path

CHEESE AND BISCUITS
Soap and cardboard

......or, for a more
interesting meal,
eat this
menu !!!

CANTEEN LADY: Do you want seconds?
PUPIL: No, thank you – I'm too young to die.

What's pink, lives on the seabed and is highly dangerous?
Al Caprawn.

What did the kipper say to the doctor?
'I'm here to be cured.'

What did they call the two monks who worked in the monastery kitchen?
The Fish Friar and the Chip Monk.

What do you get if you cross a haddock with a glove?
Fish fingers.

What is a computer's favourite food?
Silicon chips.

What is a nuclear scientist's favourite food?
Fission chips.

What's covered in cream and lives in the sea?
A jelly fish.

What's yellow and never talks to anyone?
A lemon sole.

What's yellow and white and travels at 100 mph?
A train driver's egg sandwich.

What's yellow and flat and goes around at 33⅓ revolutions per minute?
A long-playing omelette.

Why did the chicken run on to the football pitch?
Because the referee blew for a foul.

Which side of a chicken has the most feathers?
The outside.

6,743.... 6,744...
...6,745....

Did you hear about the turkey farmer who
installed a gobblestone driveway?

BERT: Why do you have carrots sticking out of
your ears?
FRED: You'll have to talk louder, I have carrots
sticking out of my ears.

'Doctor, doctor, I've got carrots growing out of
my ears!'
'How on earth did that happen?'
'I don't know – I planted cucumbers.'

What's long, orange, and shoots rabbits?
A double-barrelled carrot.

How do you find a lost rabbit?
Make a noise like a big carrot.

What's a mischievous egg called?
A practical yolker.

'Waiter, these eggs are bad.'
'Don't blame me, I only laid the table.'

Why did the egg go into the jungle?
Because it was an egg-splorer.

WAITER: We have almost everything on the menu.
RUDE BOY: So I see. Could I have a clean one, please?

Knock, knock.
  Who's there?
Martin
  Martin who?
Martin of beans won't open.

CANTEEN LADY: Eat up your spinach, it'll put colour in your cheeks.
RUDE PUPIL: Maybe, but who wants green cheeks?

Two ears of corn were running up a hill. What were they when they got to the top?
Puffed wheat.

RUDE PUPIL'S COMMENT ON CURRY:
Can I take this home in a curryer bag?

What do you get if you cross a bee with half a kilo of mince?
Humburgers.

Why was the farmer hopping mad?
Because somebody stepped on his corn.

How does a wally make scrambled eggs?
He holds the pan and gets two friends to shake him violently.

How do turkeys dance?
Chick to chick.

How can you stop a turkey gobbling on Boxing Day?
Eat him at Christmas.

Little Jack Horner sat in the corner
Eating his Christmas pie;
He put in his thumb
But instead of a plum
He squirted fruit juice in his eye.

How can you improve the taste of salt?
Sprinkle it lightly over chips.

What's yellow and highly dangerous?
A big egg-splosion.

What's yellow and even more dangerous?
An Eggs-ocet missile.

What's wet and comes out of a bottle at 100 mph?
An Aston Martini.

Where do Martians go for a drink?
A Mars bar.

What sort of tea makes you feel safe?
Safety.

What do little devils drink?
Demonade.

What is Frankenstein's favourite soup?
Scream of tomato.

HEADMASTER IN ASSEMBLY: I'm sorry to have to tell you that school meals are going up again.
PUPIL: They're difficult to keep down.

Don't eat school dinners, just throw them aside
A lot of kids didn't, a lot of kids died.
The meat's made of iron, the spuds are of steel
And if they don't kill you the pudding will.

School Cook's Favourite Recipe

A dish fit for a king (or rather, fit for a king's dustbin) . . .

Crispy Maggots in Chocolate Sauce

Ingredients:
8oz fresh writhing maggots
1 tin of dogfood
3 Mars bars
4oz squashed worms (as slimy as possible)
1oz butter or axle-grease
2oz sugar or crispy fried lice

Soak maggots thoroughly in old dishwater until they stop wriggling and float. Heat the butter in a frying pan, and fry the maggots until golden brown. Then melt the Mars bars and add the remaining ingredients. Stir well. Put the maggots in a bowl, pour over the chocolate sauce, and place in fridge until set. Serve cold with whipped toothpaste.

Why do elephants paint their toe-nails yellow?
So they can hide upside down in custard.

How can you tell when there's an elephant
hiding in your custard?
When it's especially lumpy.

What's yellow and stupid?
Thick custard.

What's yellow and highly dangerous?
A hand grenade disguised as a lemon.

What do you do with a hurt lemon?
Give it lemonade.

Why are oranges and lemons safe from pickpockets?
They don't have pockets.

What do you get when you cross an orange and a squash court?
Orange squash.

What do you get if you cross a railway engine with chewing gum?
A chew-chew train.

What's made of chocolate and rolls along the seabed?
An oyster egg.

What's woolly, covered in chocolate, and floats around the sun?
A Mars baa.

What's purple and round and floats up in the sky?
The Planet of the Grapes.

What's purple and lives in South America?
A Grape Train Robber.

What's purple and close to France?
Grape Britain.

What's purple and has eight legs?
An octoplum.

Who is purple, has scars on his head, and frightens people?
Frankenplum.

What is Dracula's favourite pudding?
Ice scream.

What pudding do you get if you cross a football team with an ice cream?
Aston Vanilla.

What do you get if you cross a granny with an ice-cream parlour?
A hot ba-nanny split.

What's yellow and has twenty-two legs?
Banana United.

What's yellow and goes thump-squish, thump-squish?
A banana with one wet plimsoll.

What's yellow and wobbly and has four wheels?
A bowl of custard on a skateboard.

What's yellow and wobbly and goes bang?
A bowl of custard in a minefield.

What's yellow and wobbly inside and white outside?
A custard sandwich.

RUDE PUPIL: Have you got any custard left?
CANTEEN LADY: Yes.
RUDE PUPIL: Well, you shouldn't have made so much then.

Why did the man have to go to hospital after the custard fell on his head?
It was in a tin.

What's yellow and wobbly and shocking?
Electric custard.

'Waiter, waiter, there's a fly in my custard!'
'Do keep quiet, or everyone will want one.'

'Waiter, waiter, there's a fly in my custard!'
'You'll have to get it out yourself, I can't swim.'

FIRST GIRL: Here, try some of this banana
custard I've just made.
SECOND GIRL: Ugh! It's horrible!
FIRST GIRL: You've no taste – it definitely says
in my cookery book that this recipe is delicious.

What happened to the criminal banana?
It was taken into custardy.

What is a banana skin most used for?
To keep the banana together.

What is a tangerine?
An orange in an easy-open wrapper.

Why did the orange go to the doctor?
Because it wasn't peeling well.

What would you do if you found a blue banana?
Try to cheer it up.

What do you get hanging from a banana tree?
Aching arms.

CANTEEN LADY: Why is your friend crying?
BOY: Because I'm eating my strawberry blancmange and I won't give him any.
CANTEEN LADY: Is his own pudding all gone?
BOY: Yes, and he cried all the time I was eating that as well.

What do you call a man with jelly in one ear and blancmange in the other?
A trifle deaf.

What sits on a shelf and wobbles?
Jellyvision.

Why did the police arrest the strawberry?
Because it was involved in a garden plot.

What's sweet and wobbles through the air?
A jellycopter.

How do you tell a peach from a Jumbo jet?
A peach's fuel tank is too small for it to cross the Atlantic without refuelling.

Why don't elephants like penguins?
Because they can't get the wrappers off.

What do you do if someone offers you rock cakes?
Take your pick.

GRANNY: What would you like?
CHILD: Cake.
GRANNY: Cake what?
CHILD: Cake first.

What's fruity and burns cakes?
Alfred the Grape.

What's fruity and burns?
The Grape Fire of London.

What's purple and ruled Russia?
Catherine the Grape.

What's purple and 8,000 kilometres long?
The Grape Wall of China.

What's round and purple and barks at people?
A Grape Dane.

How can you tell an Italian grape from one grown in Scotland?
By its suntan.

What's the definition of a raisin?
A grape with lots of worries.

What's red and miserable and covered in custard?
Apple grumble.

What's red outside, yellow inside, and very crowded?
A bus full of custard.

BOY: Can I have some custard?
CANTEEN LADY: One lump or two?

What's yellow and wobbly and moves along the bottom of the sea?
A bowl of custard in a submarine.

What's yellow and wobbly and goes round and round?
A bowl of long-playing custard.

What's yellow and wobbly and has eight
wheels?
A bowl of custard on roller skates.

What's 300 metres tall, weighs 7,620 tons, and
is made of custard?
The Trifle Tower.

'What are you doing in my apple tree, young
man?'
*'One of your apples fell down, sir, and I'm
putting it back.'*

A man saw a gardener pushing a wheelbarrow full of manure. 'Where are you going with that?' he asked. 'Going to put it on my gooseberries,' said the gardener. 'Suit yourself,' said the man, 'I usually put custard on mine.'

What's an apple that is small and yellow at picking time?
A failure.

What do you get if you cross an apple with a Christmas tree?
A pineapple.

Why are apples red?
If they were yellow they'd be lemons.

What's furry, whiskered and sucks lemons?
A sour puss.

What goes green, yellow, red, green, yellow, red, green, yellow, red?
A lemon working as a traffic light.

What is square and green?
A lemon in disguise.

What's yellow, full of seeds, and looks like half a lemon?
The other half of the lemon.

What is purple and crazy?
A grape nut.

What do you get if you cross chocolate with a madman?
A coconut.

What sits in a pram and wobbles?
A jelly baby.

How can you tell that coconut milk is nutty?
Because it lives in a padded cell.

When is a red-headed idiot like a biscuit?
When he's a ginger nut.

What's bald and wobbles?
Jelly Savalas.

What's yellow and wobbly and comes at you from all sides?
Stereophonic custard.

'Waiter, waiter, there's a fly in my custard!'
'That's all right, sir, the spider will get it.'

'Waiter, waiter, there's a fly in my custard!'
'I know, it's the rotten fruit that attracts them.'

'Waiter, waiter, there's a fly in my custard!'
'If you throw it a pea, it will play water polo.'

MAN IN RESTAURANT: Do you mind if I smoke?
RUDE BOY: Sir, I don't care if you burn.

RUDE GIRL TO SCHOOL COOK: Can you bring me some hot water please? I want to wash the cutlery.

SCHOOL COOK: I've been cooking for ten years.
RUDE PUPIL: You ought to be done by now, then.

What cake is dangerous?
Attila the Bun.

SCHOOL COOK: How do you like my cakes?
RUDE PUPIL: Delicious! Did you buy them yourself?

Should you eat twelve doughnuts on an empty stomach?
It's better to eat them on a plate.

What's sweet and swings from tree to tree?
Tarzipan.

What's sweet and fluffy and lives in the jungle?
A meringue utang.

What's white and fluffy and floats?
A cata-meringue.

What's white, creamy and always comes back to you?
A boo-meringue.

What is a lawyer's favourite pudding?
Suet.

What is Mrs Thatcher's favourite pudding?
Cabinet pudding.

What do the Scots have for pudding?
Tartan custard.

Mary had a little lamb
It leapt around in hops
It gambolled in the road one day
And finished up as chops.

Mary had a little lamb
It had a touch of colic
She gave it brandy twice a day
And now it's alcoholic.

What's yellow and wobbly and croaks?
A bowl of custard with a cold.

What happened to the man who couldn't tell
putty from custard?
His windows fell out.

What should you do if your pet plum becomes
ill?
Call a plumber.

Why is a plum a good museum keeper?
Plum preserves.

What do you get if you cross a plum and a
tiger?
A purple people eater.

What plum wrote under an alias?
Nom de plum.

What's yellow and goes click-click?
A ball-point banana.

What's enormous and yellow and says
'Fe-fi-fo-fum'?
A giant banana.

Why did the banana go out with the prune?
Because he couldn't find a date.

What's yellow and goes up and down?
A banana in a lift.

Why do boy pumpkins wear blue bow-ties?
So you can tell them from girl pumpkins.

What is an overweight pumpkin called?
A plumpkin.

Why don't grapefruit tie their own shoelaces?
*If you had a shape like a grapefruit's, you
wouldn't be able to see your feet either.*

How can you tell a pear from an elephant?
A pear always forgets.

Why do pears always forget?
What do they have to remember?

What do you get if you cross an aeroplane with
a peach tart?
Pie in the sky.

What's yellow, furry and rides along the seashore?
A peach buggy.

What's yellow, sour, and goes 'splutter, splutter, splutter'?
A lemon running out of juice.

What's yellow and goes round and round?
A long-playing lemon.

Knock, knock.
  Who's there?
Oswald.
  Oswald who?
Oswald my bubble gum.

GOBLIN YOUR FOOD IS BAD FOR YOUR ELF

Our school meals are so tough you can't even get your fork into the gravy!

MY GRANDAD OWES HIS LONG LIFE TO SCHOOL DINNERS - he never ate them!!

School food makes you SICKER QUICKER

If you put your hand in alphabet soup... ARE YOU GROPING FOR WORDS?

I DON'T LIKE CABBAGE AND I'M GLAD I DON'T LIKE IT. IF I DID LIKE IT I'D HAVE TO EAT IT, AND I HATE THE STUFF!!

What's clever, made of chocolate and travels by underground?
A tube of Smarties.

What's chocolate outside, peanut inside, and sings hymns?
A Sunday school Treet.

What's soft and pink and comes from outer space?
A Martian mellow.

What do you get if you cross an elk and a packet of cocoa?
Chocolate moose.

MOTHER: There were two bars of chocolate in the larder yesterday and now there's only one. Why?
CHILD: It must have been so dark in there I didn't see the other one.

Knock, knock.
  Who's there?
Alma.
  Alma who?
Alma sweets have gone.

What did the chocolate say to the lollipop?
'Hi, sucker.'

What do bees do with honey?
They cell it.

Knock, knock.
    Who's there?
Pear.
    Pear who?
Pear of shoes.

Knock, knock.
    Who's there?
Shoes
    Shoes who?
Shoes me, I didn't mean to tread on your pear.

What does God eat for tea?
Angel cakes.

What do you get if you cross a citrus fruit with a bell?
An orange that can peal itself.

What do you get if you cross a duck with a cow?
Cream quackers.

What do you get if you cross a hammer with a biscuit?
Crumbs.

Why did the apple turnover?
Because it saw the Swiss roll.

How can you tell that a wedding cake is sad?
Because of its tiers.

Why wouldn't the man eat apples?
Because his granny had died of apple-plexy.

'Mum, can I have 20p for the old man crying outside in the street?'
'Of course, son. What is he crying about?'
'Toffee apples – 20p each.'

Confucius, he say: An apple a day keeps the doctor away – if aimed correctly.

What animals in Noah's Ark didn't come in pairs?
Worms – they came in apples.

What lives in apples and is an avid reader?
A bookworm.

What is a prickly pear?
Two porcupines.

MAN IN RESTAURANT: Do you mind if I smoke?
RUDE GIRL: Not if you don't mind me being sick.

RUDE GIRL: Are waiters supposed to be tipped?
WAITER: Of course.
RUDE GIRL: Good, then tip me. I've been waiting for service for half an hour.

I sat next to a duchess at tea
And it was as I feared it would be;
Her rumblings abdominal
Were simply phenomenal
And everyone thought it was me.

If you have a referee in boxing, a referee in football, and a referee in rugby, what do you have in bowls?
Custard.

'Waiter, waiter, there's a fly in my custard!'
'Don't worry, I'll send for the RSPCA.'

'Waiter, waiter, there's a fly in my custard!'
'No, sir, that's the chef – the last customer was a witch doctor.'

What's purple and swings through the trees?
Tarzan of the Grapes.

What's purple and glows in the dark?
A 100 watt grape.

What American lakes are filled with purple juice?
The Grape Lakes.

Who was purple and discovered America in 1492?
Christopher Plumbus.

What did the biscuit say when it was run over?
'Oh crumbs.'

How can you tell that strawberries are lazy?
Because they spend their entire lives in bed.

What did the girl say after she ate a whole basket of fresh peaches?
'Burp!'

What is the difference between a lemon and a melon?
The order in which their letters are written.

What's yellow, wears a cape, and fights crime?
Superbanana.

What's yellow and wobbly and wears dark glasses?
A bowl of custard in disguise.

What's yellow and jumps up and down?
A banana at a disco.

What do you get if you cross a sheepdog and a bowl of custard?
Collie-wobbles.

Knock, knock.
Who's there?
Dishes.
Dishes who?
Dishes the very last knock-knock in this book.

Why did the baker stop making doughnuts?
Because he got tired of the whole business.

Should you eat twelve doughnuts on an empty stomach?
It's better to eat them on a plate.

COOKERY TEACHER: How do you make a Swiss roll?
PUPIL: Push him down an Alp.

To be sung to the tune of Frère Jacques:
School dinners! School dinners!
Concrete chips! Concrete chips!
Semolina pudding, semolina pudding,
I feel sick, bathroom quick!

Bookworm's Banquet

- ★ *Food on my Plate* by E Tittup
- ★ *Choosing the Best Meat* by Selena Cut
- ★ *Fast Food* by MacDonald and Ken Tucky
- ★ *Make Your Own Gobstoppers* by Annie Seed
- ★ *How to Run a Snackbar* by Sam Witch and Chick N N Amme
- ★ *Morning Break* by T N Bikkies
- ★ *Healthy Salads* by Tom Ato, Walter Cress and B Trute
- ★ *Vegetable Soups* by Minny Strony and Molly Gert Awny
- ★ *Rice Growing* by Paddy Fields
- ★ *The British Breakfast* by Chris P Bacon and Hammond Eggs
- ★ *Delicious Fish* by Hal E Butt, Ann Chovee, Sam Monn, Y Ting and C Bass
- ★ *Where to Buy Exotic Food* by Della Cattesson
- ★ *The Ice Cream Man* by Alick Malolli
- ★ *The Perfect Cuppa* by T Striner
- ★ *Home Baking* by Victoria Spongecake
- ★ *Casserole Cookery* by Stewart Slowly
- ★ *How to be Slim* by Anita Figure
- ★ *Know Your Vegetables* by P Zargreen
- ★ *The Fry Up* by Egon Cheeps

- ★ *Grow Your Own Vegetables* by R T Choke
- ★ *How to Serve Minestrone* by Sue Playdell
- ★ *Middle Eastern Cookery* by Donna Kebabs
- ★ *Eat Like a Rabbit* by Norah Lettisleefe